Thanksgiving Day

Dianne M. MacMillan

Reading Consultant:

Michael P. French, Ph.D.
Bowling Green State University

—Best Holiday Books—

Enslow Publishers, Inc.

44 Fadem Road   PO Box 38
Box 699   Aldershot
Springfield, NJ 07081   Hants GU12 6BP
USA   UK

*To my sister Fran, who always makes
Thanksgiving Day special.*

Acknowledgments
*The author would like to thank Maxine N. Lurie,
professor of American history, Seton Hall University, for
her careful review of the manuscript.*

Copyright © 1997 by Enslow Publishers, Inc.

Library of Congress Cataloging-in-Publication Data

MacMillan, Dianne.
    Thanksgiving Day / Dianne M. MacMillan.
      p. cm. — (Best holiday books)
    Includes index.
    Summary: Describes the history of Thanksgiving Day, how it
came to be celebrated on the fourth Thursday in November, and
the traditions associated with this holiday.
    ISBN 0-89490-822-7
    1. Thanksgiving Day—History—Juvenile literature. 2. United States—
Social life and customs—Juvenile literature. [1. Thanksgiving Day.]
I. Title. II. Series.
GT4975.M3 1997
394.2'649'0973—dc20

                           96-31395
                           CIP
                           AC

Printed in the United States of America

10 9 8 7 6 5 4 3 2 1

Illustration Credits: Dianne M. MacMillan, pp. 4, 22; Mrs. Kevin Scheibel, pp. 6, 16,
21, 35, 37, 38, 42, 43; Library of Congress, pp. 10, 13, 15, 17, 25, 27; Macy's
Thanksgiving Day Parade, pp. 30, 41; Tom McCarthy/Unicorn Photos, p. 44; Wilma
Willis Gore, pp. 33, 36.

Cover Illustration: Mrs. Kevin Scheibel

Contents

Family and friends gather together to share Thanksgiving dinner.

We Gather Together

Delicious, mouthwatering smells of pie, sweet potatoes, and roast turkey fill the kitchen. Everyone is busy helping to get the meal ready. Meanwhile, children watch for family and friends to arrive. Excitement fills the air. Soon everyone will sit down together to share dinner. Today is the fourth Thursday in November. All across our land people gather together to celebrate Thanksgiving. It has been done for over three hundred years.

Some families go to church or synagogue to thank God for their blessings. Others offer a special prayer before the meal. It is a time for

Many Americans say a special prayer before eating. They thank God for all of their blessings.

sharing good food and rejoicing with family and friends. The idea of giving thanks is not new.

Thousands of years ago people gave thanks for a good harvest. Romans held a harvest feast. They thanked Ceres, the goddess of grain and wheat.

Ancient Greeks also had days of thanksgiving for a good harvest. Each year Hebrews celebrated the harvest feast of Sukkot for seven days.

People all over the world celebrate days of thanksgiving. The United States was the first country to make Thanksgiving Day a national holiday. How did this celebration begin?

The First Thanksgiving

In the early 1600s some Christians in England were called Puritans. Puritans believed that the Bible was the "pure" word of God. Some of the Puritans grew unhappy with the Church of England. They wanted to make changes. The king would not allow the changes.

This group of Puritans broke from the church. They called themselves Separatists because they separated or broke away. King James I was angry with the Separatists. He believed that they were enemies. He ordered his soldiers to arrest, jail, and fine them.

Some of the Separatists escaped to Holland.

There, they lived in peace. However, they could not get good jobs. As the years passed the Separatists grew unhappy. Some of their children were forgetting English customs. The Separatists wanted a new life in a place where they could worship God in their own way.

The Separatists asked for permission to settle in the Virginia colony in the new world. The London Company had been given a grant by the king to settle the colony. Jamestown, Virginia, was the first settlement. The London Company gave the Separatists permission to start another settlement in Virginia.

The Separatists were poor. They did not have enough money to make the trip. Seventy English businessmen formed a partnership with the Separatists. The men agreed to pay for the ship, crew, and settlement. Later the Separatists would send lumber, furs, and fish back to England.

Some of the Separatists living in Holland would sail to America. The rest would follow in a few years. William Bradford, one of the leaders, would go with the first group. As they prepared to leave Holland, Bradford wrote in his journal, "they knew they were pilgrims. . . ."

On September 16, 1620, fifty men, twenty women, and thirty-two children crowded into a tiny ship called the *Mayflower*. They set sail from Plymouth, England. Not all of the 102 passengers were Separatists. Twenty-five were

The *Mayflower* carried 102 passengers on the journey across the Atlantic Ocean.

crew members. There were also soldiers, servants, and craftsmen.

William Bradford called the forty-one Separatists "saints." All of the other passengers were called "strangers." Everyone on this voyage later became known as Pilgrims because they were wandering far from home. Captain Myles Standish was in charge of the soldiers. He went along to protect the Pilgrims from danger in their new settlement.

At first the ocean was calm. Then the weather changed. The tiny ship rocked and tossed in the waves. It rode out storm after storm. Many of the Pilgrims were seasick. They spent the long days praying, singing, and reading the Bible.

The Pilgrims and ship's crew ate hard biscuits and dried food. Day after day they continued their journey. One man died. A new baby was born. His parents named him Oceanus.

On November 11, after sixty-six days, they sighted land near Cape Cod, Massachusetts. They were a long way from Virginia. The storms had blown the tiny ship off course. With winter coming, they decided to settle in the New England area.

Captain Standish and his men went ashore in a small boat called a shallop. They searched for the best area for the Pilgrims to settle. After four weeks they chose a site.

Because this land was not a part of Virginia, it was not controlled by the London Company. So before landing, the Pilgrim men signed a paper. This paper was called the Mayflower Compact. It was an agreement about their new government. It promised that the "saints" and "strangers" would have equal laws. The agreement said that they could choose their own governor. The Pilgrims chose John Carver to be their first governor.

In December the first Pilgrims went ashore. Years earlier the English explorer Captain John Smith had named this place Plimouth. On the shore there was a large rock. They did not know it, but the rock had come from a glacier millions of years ago.

It was the beginning of winter. The Pilgrims

arrived in a freezing rain storm. Even though the weather was fierce, men began cutting down trees. Logs were dragged and cut by hand.

The men hammered the cut logs together to build the first shelter. It was a large meeting house. It would be used also as a church and as a fort. Some of the Pilgrims lived in the meeting house until their homes could be built.

Women and children slept on the *Mayflower.*

The Pilgrims landed in Plymouth in late 1620.

The weather was bitterly cold. Many Pilgrims became sick and died.

When spring arrived the weather grew warmer. Only fifty-seven Pilgrims were still alive. Many of the women had died. Only four remained. Twenty-three children survived. The Pilgrims did not have the skills to survive in the wilderness. They did not know how to farm this land. Many of the seeds that they brought from England would not grow. Some of the craftsmen did not know how to hunt or fish. The future of the Pilgrims looked bleak.

One day a tall Native American by the name of Samoset walked into their settlement. He greeted them in English. The Pilgrims were amazed. Samoset explained that he had learned English from fishermen along the coast of Maine. Samoset brought his chief, Massasoit, to meet the Pilgrims.

A week later Samoset returned with another Native American, Tisquantum. Tisquantum also spoke English. Tisquantum stayed to help the Pilgrims. They called him Squanto.

In April, the *Mayflower* and its crew returned to England. None of the Pilgrims sailed with the ship. They were determined to make a home in this new place. Governor Carver died in May. The Pilgrims named William Bradford as their new governor.

Squanto taught the Pilgrims how to plant corn, pumpkins, and squash. These vegetables

Chief Massasoit meets with the Pilgrims and Governor Carver.

Native Americans showed the Pilgrims how to grow pumpkins.

were new to the Pilgrims. In the forest he showed the men how to hunt deer, turkey, and catch fish in local streams. He showed the children where to gather wild berries.

Squanto knew the area very well. The Pilgrims had chosen the same site that Squanto's village had stood on years before. All the other members of his village had died from a disease. Without Squanto's knowledge and help, the

Pilgrims might not have survived. Squanto also helped the Pilgrims make a peace treaty with the other tribes in the area. Governor Bradford wrote in his journal that Squanto, "was a special instrument sent of God for (our) good."

In the fall of 1621 the harvest was plentiful. The Pilgrims wanted to celebrate. Governor Bradford asked Squanto to invite Chief Massasoit and a few friends to a feast. Instead of a few friends, Chief Massasoit arrived with

On the first Thanksgiving, the Pilgrims and Native Americans feasted and played games.

ninety men! Fortunately Massasoit also brought five deer. There was plenty of food. The Pilgrims and Native Americans ate turkey, deer, fish, corn, pumpkins, squash, plums, and other berries. Four women, with help from the children, did all the cooking.

For three days the Pilgrims and Native Americans feasted and played games. They held foot races and jumping contests. The soldiers under Captain Standish marched and fired their rifles. The Pilgrims called the celebration a harvest feast. It reminded them of their harvest festival held in England each year.

The Pilgrims did not call this celebration Thanksgiving. To them, a day of thanksgiving was a day spent praying and fasting. Fasting means not to eat any food. They would hold a Thanksgiving Day of prayer and fasting two years later.

However, as years passed, Americans read and learned about this first harvest feast. People called the celebration shared by the Native Americans and Pilgrims the first Thanksgiving.

Many Days of Thanksgiving

For the next one hundred and fifty years, thanksgiving days were celebrated whenever a minister or governor would set aside a special day. It could be any day of the week or year. More often than not, Thursday was a favorite day. This day did not interfere with the Sabbath.

Many New England colonies combined the idea of a day of prayer and giving thanks with a feast. They celebrated an annual fall Thanksgiving Day. For a long time the idea was not popular with the southern colonies.

During the American Revolution (1776–1783), the Continental Congress proclaimed a day of praise and thanksgiving for all thirteen states. It was held on December 18, 1777. The day was set aside to pray and thank God. Other celebrations were held in 1781, 1783, and 1784—usually after a battle victory. Sometimes these days were in October; other times, in December.

President George Washington proclaimed two special days of thanksgiving and praise during the 1790s. Still, he did not make the holiday an annual one.

Meanwhile, the New England states continued to celebrate an annual Thanksgiving Day. They held it each fall on a Thursday, just as they had done during the colonial times. The day began with everyone going to church. The minister read a Thanksgiving message from the state governor. After spending several hours in church everyone went home to dinner.

For weeks families prepared for the feast. Instead of serving one kind of meat, New Englanders served five or six: turkey, chicken, roasted ducks and geese, along with lamb, pork,

Many people go to church or synagogue on Thanksgiving Day to thank God for their blessings.

Delicious pies are a favorite dessert.

or beef. They also ate a variety of vegetables and many different kinds of pies.

As our country grew, people from New England moved to new states in the west. They took their tradition of Thanksgiving Day with them. States held their Thanksgiving on different days. Thanksgiving Day might come in September or even in January.

Many people felt that Thanksgiving Day was special. They wanted to have an annual holiday with everyone in the country celebrating on the same day.

People who celebrated the holiday needed someone to take charge. They needed someone to convince the government to proclaim one annual Thanksgiving Day for the entire United States. The person most responsible for doing that was a woman named Sarah Josepha Hale. Many call her the "Mother of Thanksgiving."

Sarah Josepha Hale

Sarah Josepha Buell was born in New Hampshire in 1788. She grew up with two older brothers and a younger sister. Each year her favorite holiday was Thanksgiving Day. She and her brothers and sister looked forward to the day. They helped their parents prepare all the food and get ready for the feast.

In 1813 Sarah married David Hale. Together they had five children. Nine years later her husband died suddenly. Sarah Hale became a writer to support her family. Writing was one of the few ways a woman could support herself in the 1800s. Her first novel was called

Northwood: Life North and South. In one chapter she wrote about how New Englanders celebrate Thanksgiving. She wrote, "Thanksgiving like the Fourth of July, should be considered a national holiday and observed by all people."

Sarah Josepha Hale helped make Thanksgiving Day an annual holiday.

The novel was successful. Soon Hale was given the job as editor of the *Ladies' Magazine* in Boston. Later she became editor of *Godey's Lady's Book*. For the next twenty years it was the most widely read magazine in the country.

Each fall Hale printed stories and poems about Thanksgiving Day. The magazine included recipes. It gave readers directions on how to stuff a turkey and bake a pie. But Hale was not content with writing columns about Thanksgiving Day. She began to write letters about Thanksgiving.

Starting in 1846 she wrote to every state and territorial governor. She urged each of them to proclaim the last Thursday in November as Thanksgiving Day. Through the years she also wrote to each United States president. Sarah refused to give up and wrote more than one thousand letters. As a result, more and more governors proclaimed a day of Thanksgiving for their states.

During the Civil War (1861–1865), both the North and the South proclaimed special days of thanksgiving after important victories. On

President Lincoln proclaimed Thanksgiving Day a national holiday in 1863.

September 28, 1863, Sarah Josepha Hale wrote to President Abraham Lincoln asking him to make Thanksgiving Day a national holiday.

Lincoln invited Hale to visit him. He liked her idea very much. He proclaimed the last Thursday of November 1863 as Thanksgiving Day for the entire nation. Sarah Josepha Hale had succeeded in making Thanksgiving Day a holiday for everyone.

The Holiday Grows and Changes

Over the next fifty years Thanksgiving became more popular around the country. Then in 1921 Gimbel's department store in Philadelphia held the first Thanksgiving Day parade. Gimbel's hoped the parade would kick off the Christmas holiday season. The store owners wanted to remind people to start shopping for Christmas presents. The parade was a huge success.

Three years later, in 1924, Macy's department store in New York City held its first Thanksgiving Day Parade. Ten thousand people

Getting Ready

Today it is easier to prepare Thanksgiving dinner than during the time of the Pilgrims. Families no longer have to shoot a wild turkey for dinner. Turkey farms raise thousands and thousands of turkeys for the holiday. Grocery stores stock up on pumpkins, sweet potatoes, and other fruits and vegetables. Planning and shopping for the meal is still a big event. Children love to help cook the dinner.

The week before Thanksgiving Day, many boys and girls put on school plays about the first Thanksgiving. Children dress up in Pilgrim and Native American costumes. Students make turkeys out of construction paper and decorate bulletin boards. They read Thanksgiving poems and stories. Magazines have plenty of recipes on cooking Thanksgiving dinner just as they did years ago when Sarah Josepha Hale was an editor.

A fun thing to do is visit a living history museum. Plimouth Plantation located near Plymouth, Massachusetts, re-creates actual life

Turkey farms raise thousands of turkeys for the holiday.

in seventeenth-century Plymouth. People dress in Pilgrim and Native American costumes. They do chores just as the Pilgrims did. The women tend the gardens. The men harvest and thrash the grain. You can talk to them about the harvest celebration in 1621.

Nearby the *Mayflower II* is anchored. It is a reproduction of the ship that carried the Pilgrims to the New World. It was built in England. On April 20, 1957, it sailed from Plymouth, England, to Plymouth Harbor in Massachusetts. On board, actors play the parts of the Pilgrims and crew members that made the voyage. After visiting the museum you can understand what life was like for the Pilgrims.

On the shore near the harbor is the large granite rock. It is called Plymouth Rock. Some stories say that the Pilgrims stepped on it when they landed. These stories are untrue. Probably the Pilgrims used the rock as a landmark. It might have guided them into the harbor. Visitors love to see this ancient piece of rock.

Families enjoy spending time together on

For thousands of years people have given thanks for a good harvest.

Thanksgiving Day. Each year millions of people climb on buses, trains, planes, and into cars, to share Thanksgiving with their families. The day before Thanksgiving is the busiest travel day of the year in our country.

Another part of Thanksgiving is the spirit of sharing with others less fortunate. Many churches and community groups prepare Thanksgiving dinner for poor and homeless people. Most Americans are happy to give food

This mother is showing her sons the roast turkey for dinner.

The day before Thanksgiving Day is the busiest travel day of the year.

Boxes of food are donated to the poor at Thanksgiving time.

and money to help others. They want everyone to have a joyful Thanksgiving.

People who live in Canada celebrate Thanksgiving Day on the second Monday in October. The Canadian Thanksgiving had its beginning forty-five years before the Pilgrim celebration.

The English explorer Martin Frobisher tried to find a passage to India. His fifteen ships had a difficult and rough journey. The explorers thought that they would all drown at sea. Then in 1578 they landed on Baffin Island in Canada.

The men celebrated with a prayer service. They thanked God for their safe trip. After prayers they feasted on local wildlife and fish. Canada made Thanksgiving a national holiday in 1879.

We Give Thanks

Finally, the big day is here. Schools and most businesses are closed. Each year the president of the United States gives a special Thanksgiving message, just as President Washington did many years ago. His message is printed in newspapers. Thanksgiving parades are held in large cities.

The Macy's Thanksgiving Day Parade has become a part of our tradition. It is viewed on television by over 60 million people. The parade is most famous for its giant helium balloons. The balloons are three stories tall and move slowly down the streets. The parade also has floats carrying people who sing and wave to the crowd.

Santa's Sleigh is the last float in Macy's Thanksgiving Day Parade.

Santa Claus rides on the last float, signaling the parade's end.

In the early 1800s baseball games were played on Thanksgiving Day. For the past one hundred years football has been the Thanksgiving sport played most often. High school, college, as well as professional teams, all play that day. The players are carrying on the tradition of playing games that was started by the Pilgrims and Native Americans.

The highlight of the day is when everyone sits

Football is the sport played most often on Thanksgiving Day.

The turkey is roasted to a golden brown color. It is time to EAT!

down at the table for dinner. This is the moment. The turkey is roasted to a golden brown color. Family and friends crowd around the table. It is time to carve the turkey. Many Americans say a special Thanksgiving prayer before dinner. They thank God for the good food, their families, and all their blessings.

Then it is time to EAT! Each family has its

own special dishes and traditional foods. Some make candied sweet potatoes, creamed onions, or jellied cranberries. Others have a favorite stuffing. It might be oyster, chestnut, sage, sausage, or mushroom. Regardless of the stuffing, many families will eat turkey, pumpkin, and corn. They are carrying on the tradition begun long ago by the Pilgrims and Native Americans. HAPPY THANKSGIVING!

This family is celebrating Thanksgiving Day just as Americans have done for hundreds of years.

Glossary

Continental Congress—A group of men from each of the colonies that came together to plan the colonists' opposition to England's laws.

editor—A person who corrects and checks written work before it is printed in a book, magazine, or newspaper.

glacier—A large mass of ice formed by snow that does not melt. Long ago glaciers covered much of North America.

journal—A written daily record or account.

minister—A teacher of religion; a preacher.

New England—The six northeast states of the United States: Maine, Vermont, New Hampshire, Massachusetts, Rhode Island, and Connecticut.

pilgrim—A person who travels far from his or her home.

proclaim—To announce publicly.

Puritan—Protestant reformers who wanted to "purify" or reform the Church of England.

Sabbath—The day of the week that is used for worship.

Separatists—The Puritans who broke away from the Church of England.

shallop—A sailboat carried on the *Mayflower*. It was used for exploring the coast.

tradition—To do the same thing in the same way every year.

United States Congress—The branch of the United States government that makes laws.

Index